Maria Dia

CW00749811

CROSS STITCH MOTIF SERIES 5
KANAVIÇE MOTIF SERISI 5

LANDSCAPES
MANZARALAR

50 New Cross Stitch Models
50 Yeni Kanaviçe Modeli

TUVA
Yayıncılık

Tuva Yayıncılık / Tuva Publishing
www.tuvayayincilik.com

Adres / Address: Merkez Mah. Çavuşbaşı Cad. No:71
Çekmeköy / Istanbul 34782 - TURKEY
Tel: 9 0216 642 62 62

Kanaviçe Motif Serisi 5 / Manzaralar
Cross Stitch Motif Series 5 / Landscapes

İlk Basım / First Print: 2012 / Aralık - December, Istanbul
İkinci Basım / Second Print: 2013 /Mayıs - May - Istanbul

Dünyadaki tüm hakları - All Global Copyrights Belongs To
Tuva Tekstil San. ve Dış Tic. Ltd. Şti.

Konusu / Content: Kanaviçe - Cross Stitch

Yayın Yönetmeni / Editor in Chief: Ayhan DEMİRPEHLİVAN
Proje Editörü / Project Editor: Kader DEMİRPEHLİVAN
Tasarımcı / Designer: Maria DIAZ
Teknik Danışman / Technical Advisor: K. Leyla ARAS
Grafik / Graphic Design: Ömer ALP, Büşra ESER
Asistan / Asistant: Kevser BAYRAKÇI

Tüm hakları saklıdır. Bu yayının hiçbir bölümü yayıncıdan yazılı olarak öncelikli izin alınmadan herhangi bir şekilde ve herhangi bir amaçla yeniden çoğaltılamaz, elektronik veya mekanik olarak; fotokopi, kayıt cihazı ve diğer yollarla geri erişim sistemlerinde depolanamaz veya yayınlanamaz. Bu kitaptaki tasarımların telif hakları korunmaktadır ve ticari amaçla kullanılamaz.

All rights reserved. No part of this publication shall be reproduced by any means and for any purpose, stored or published electronically or mechanically, in retrieval engines as photocopy, through recorder or other means without prior written consent of the publisher. The copyrights of the designs in this book are protected and shall not be used for any commercial purpose.

ISBN: 978-605-5647-40-7

Basıldığı Matbaa / Printing House
Bilnet Matbaacılık - Biltur Yayın ve Hizmet A.Ş. Dudullu
Organize Sanayi Bölgesi 1. Cadde No:16 - Ümraniye - Istanbul / Turkey
Tel: 9 0216 444 44 03

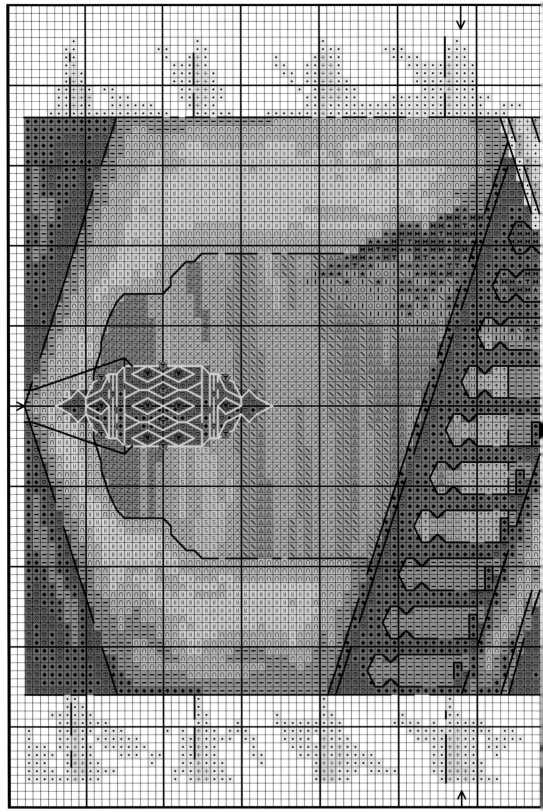

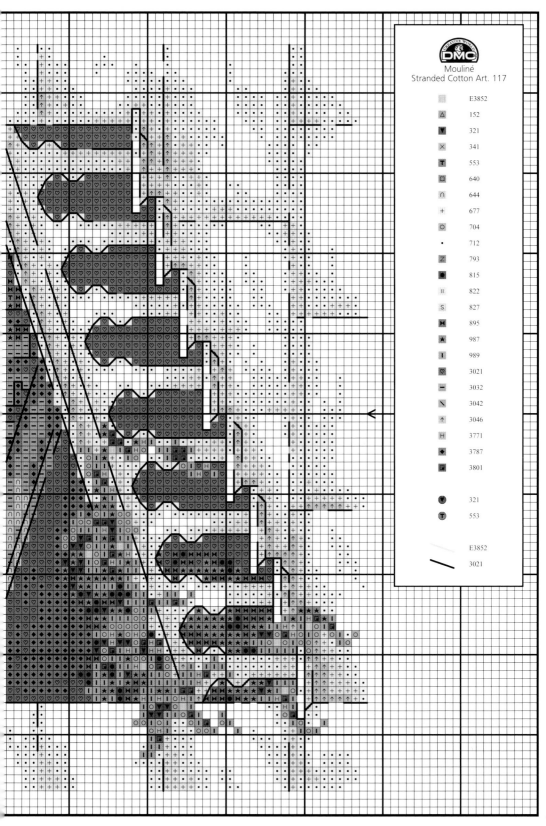

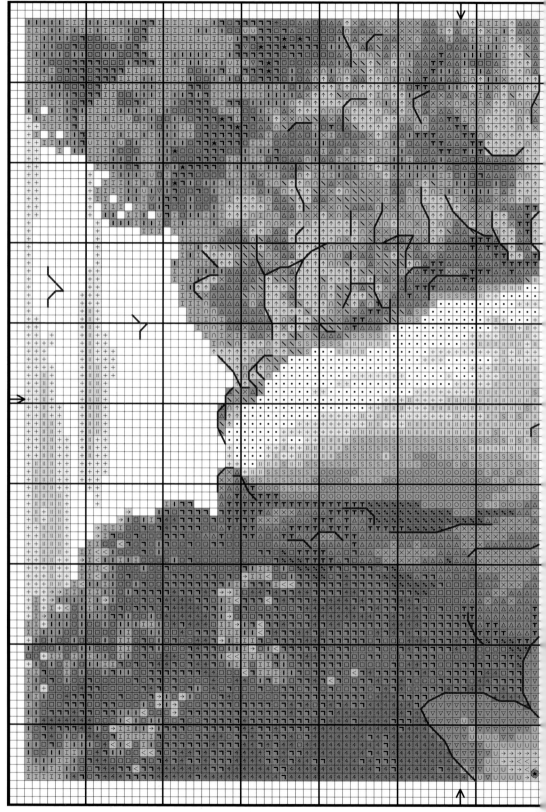

8

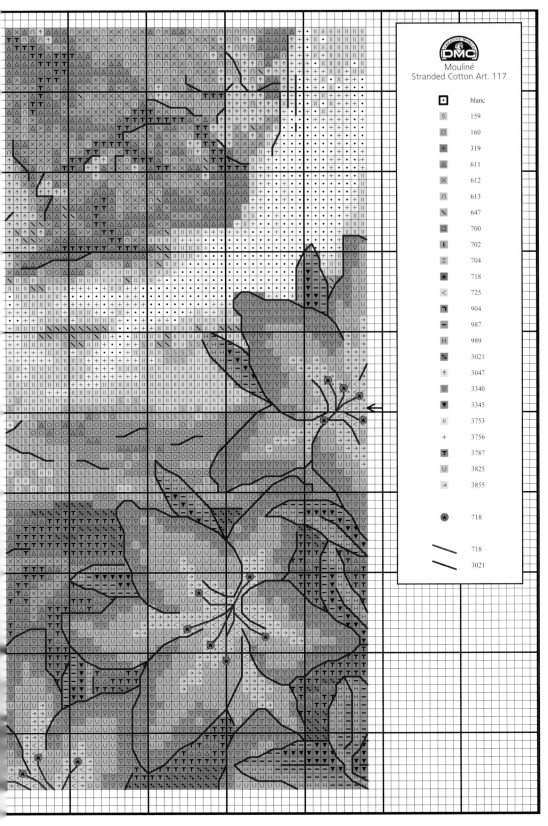

	DMC
	Mouliné
	Stranded Cotton Art. 117
▣	blanc
S	159
O	160
✠	319
△	611
✕	612
∩	613
＼	647
▢	700
Ⅰ	702
Ⅰ	704
✦	718
<	725
⊓	904
━	987
H	989
✖	3021
↑	3047
▽	3340
▼	3345
‖	3753
+	3756
T	3787
U	3825
→	3855
★	718
/	718
/	3021

9

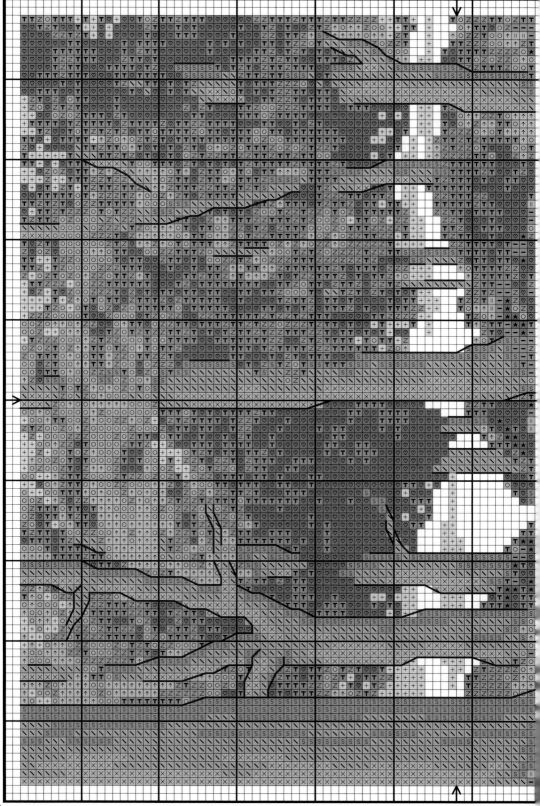

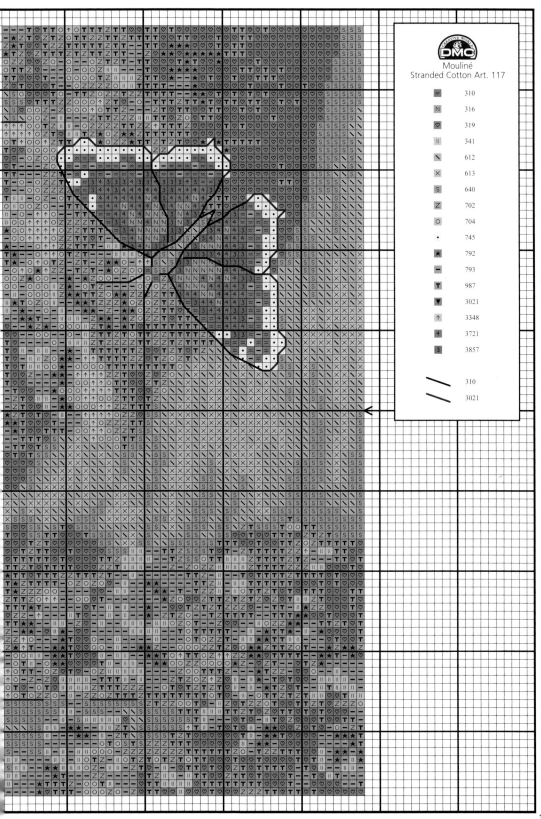

≡	310
N	316
♡	319
‖	341
\	612
✕	613
S	640
Z	702
O	704
·	745
★	792
−	793
T	987
▼	3021
↑	3348
4	3721
3	3857
/	310
/	3021

Mouliné
Stranded Cotton Art. 117

DMC
Mouliné
Stranded Cotton Art. 117

⊡	blanc
<	162
▣	317
N	318
U	415
I	435
Z	640
—	642
S	644
X	738
+	762
★	801
T	930
◪	3371
▼	3799
O	3864
╱	3371

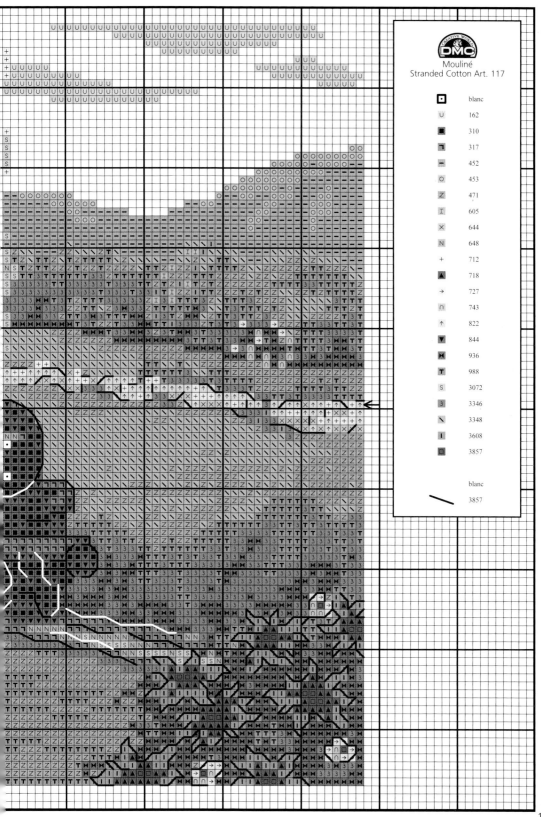

	DMC
	Mouliné
	Stranded Cotton Art. 117
▣	blanc
U	162
■	310
◥	317
▬	452
O	453
Z	471
I	605
×	644
N	648
+	712
▲	718
→	727
∩	743
↑	822
▼	844
⋈	936
T	988
S	3072
3	3346
⟍	3348
I	3608
▣	3857
	blanc
╱	3857

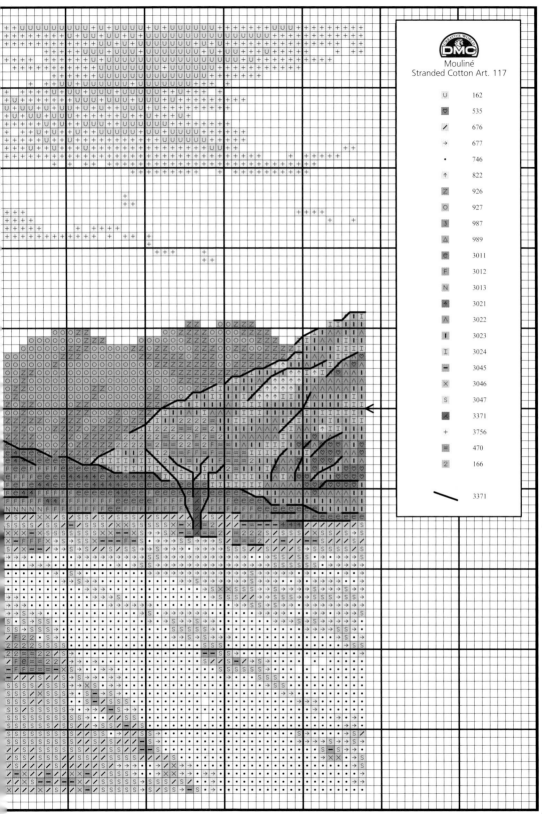

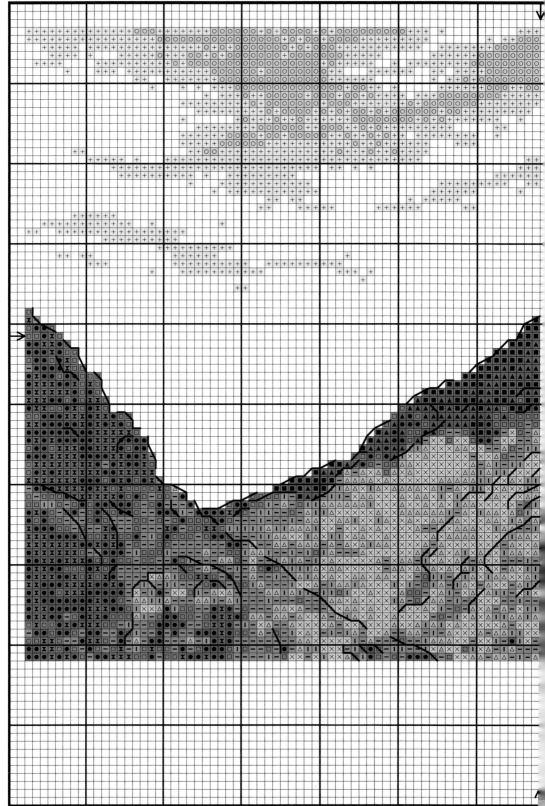

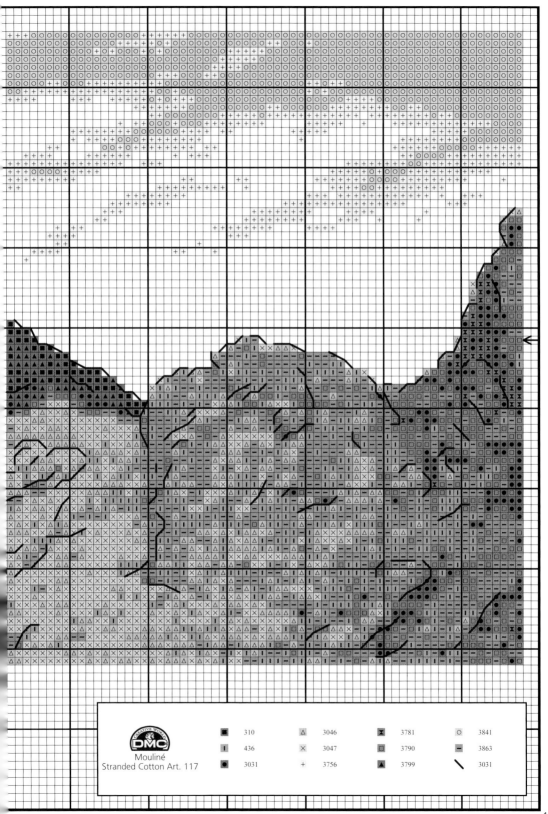

■	310	△	3046	✕	3781	○	3841
I	436	✕	3047	▣	3790	−	3863
●	3031	+	3756	▲	3799	╱	3031

DMC
CREATIVE WORLD
Mouliné
Stranded Cotton Art. 117

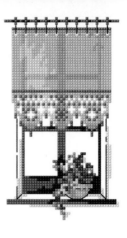

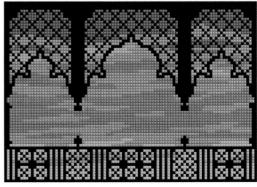

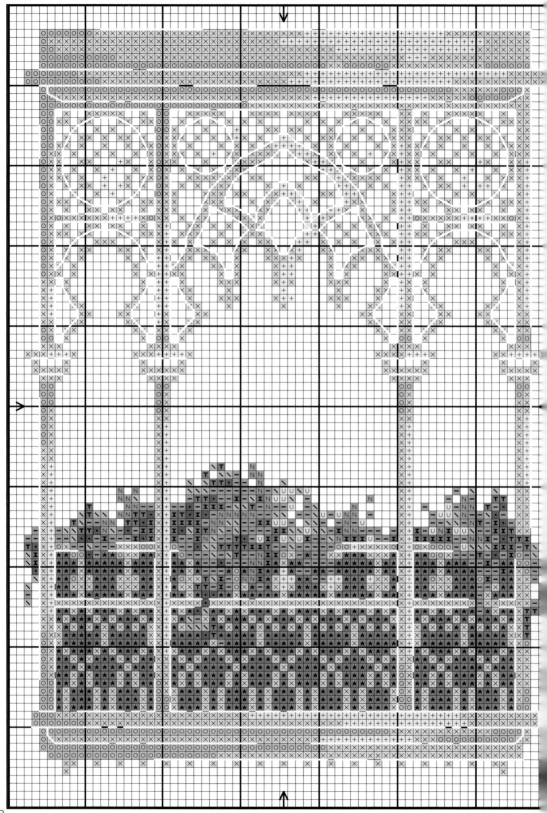

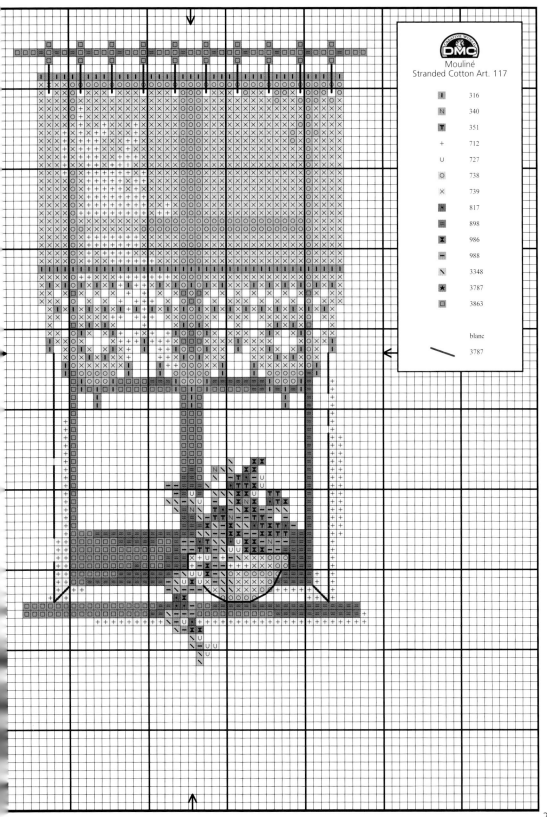

I	316
N	340
T	351
+	712
U	727
O	738
X	739
	817
	898
	986
	988
	3348
	3787
	3863
	blanc
	3787

Mouliné
Stranded Cotton Art. 117

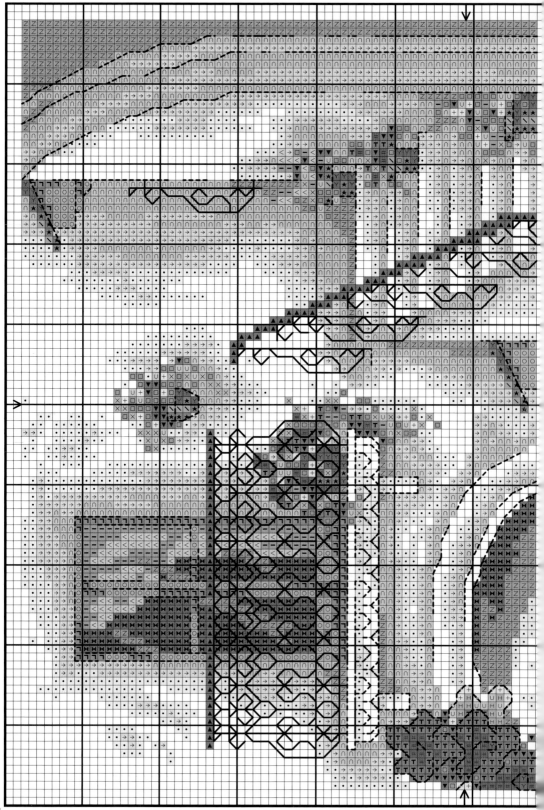

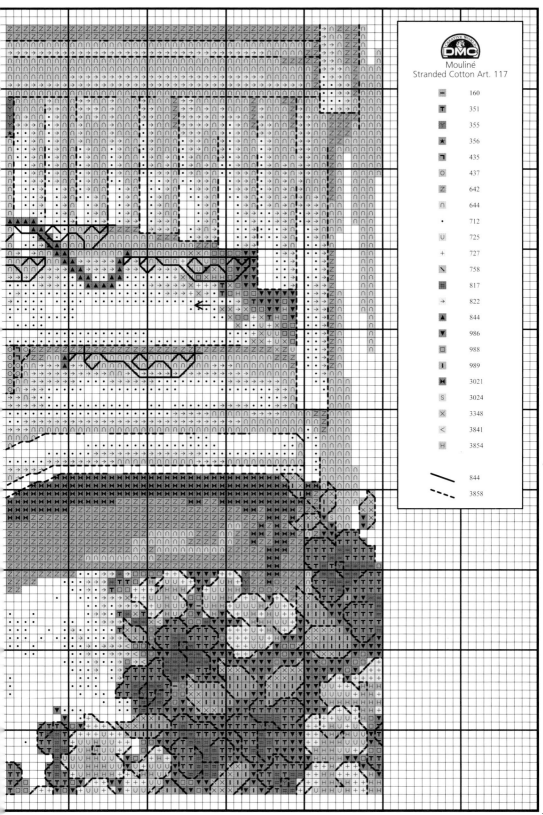

DMC
Mouliné
Stranded Cotton Art. 117

Symbol	Code
–	160
T	351
Y	355
★	356
⊓	435
o	437
Z	642
∩	644
•	712
U	725
+	727
⊡	758
⊞	817
→	822
▲	844
▼	986
□	988
I	989
⋈	3021
S	3024
X	3348
<	3841
H	3854
──	844
---	3858

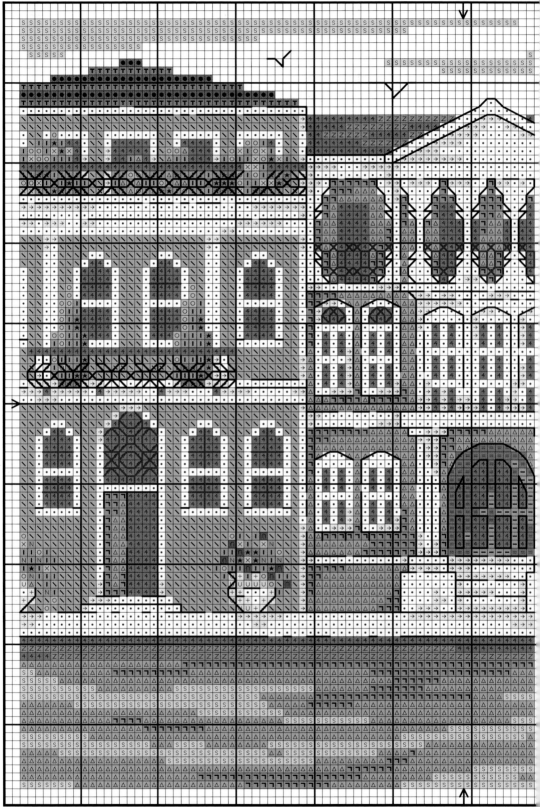

DMC
Mouliné
Stranded Cotton Art. 117

⊡	blanc
S	162
≡	301
●	355
T	356
─	436
Z	646
+	712
U	739
N	741
✕	743
N	758
→	762
△	813
n	817
4	844
⅂	931
I	988
★	3346
O	3348
╱	blanc
╱	844

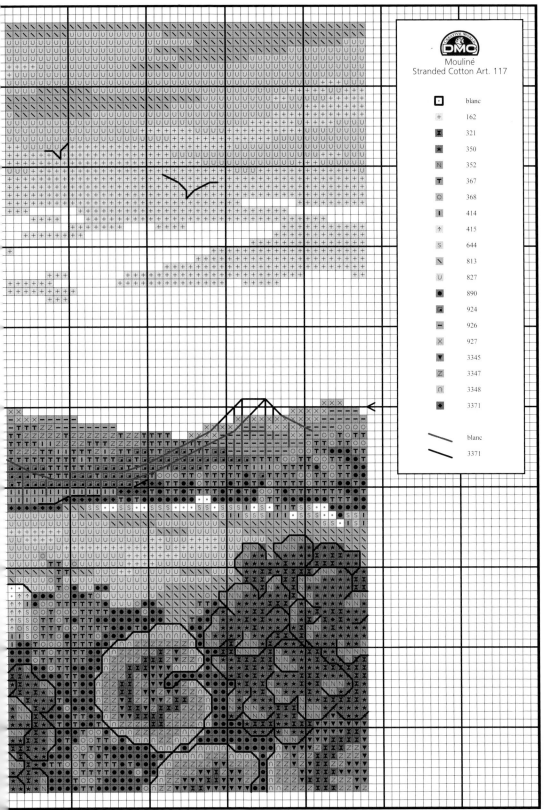

DMC
Mouliné
Stranded Cotton Art. 117

☐	blanc
+	162
✕	321
★	350
N	352
T	367
○	368
I	414
↑	415
S	644
＼	813
U	827
●	890
▣	924
━	926
✕	927
▼	3345
Z	3347
∩	3348
✦	3371

╱	blanc
╱	3371

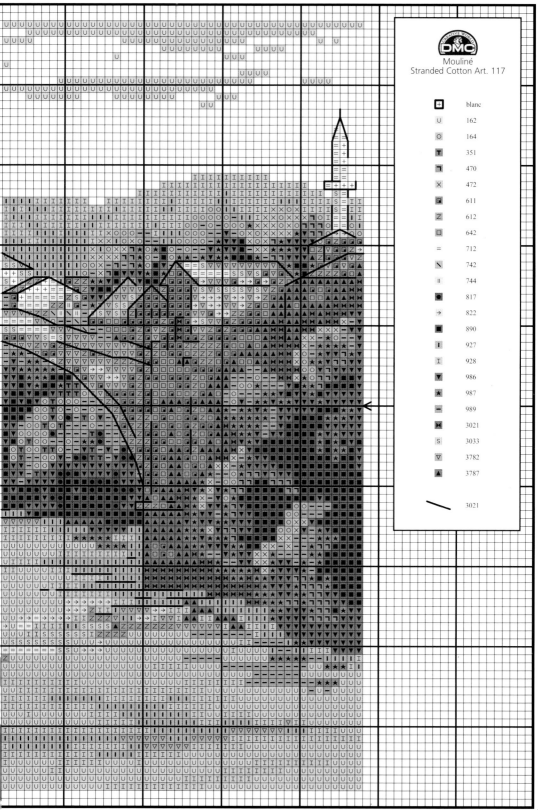

DMC
Mouliné
Stranded Cotton Art. 117

⊞	blanc
U	162
O	164
T	351
⌐	470
×	472
▣	611
Z	612
▢	642
=	712
◥	742
‖	744
●	817
→	822
■	890
I	927
I	928
▼	986
★	987
—	989
◄	3021
S	3033
▽	3782
▲	3787
╱	3021

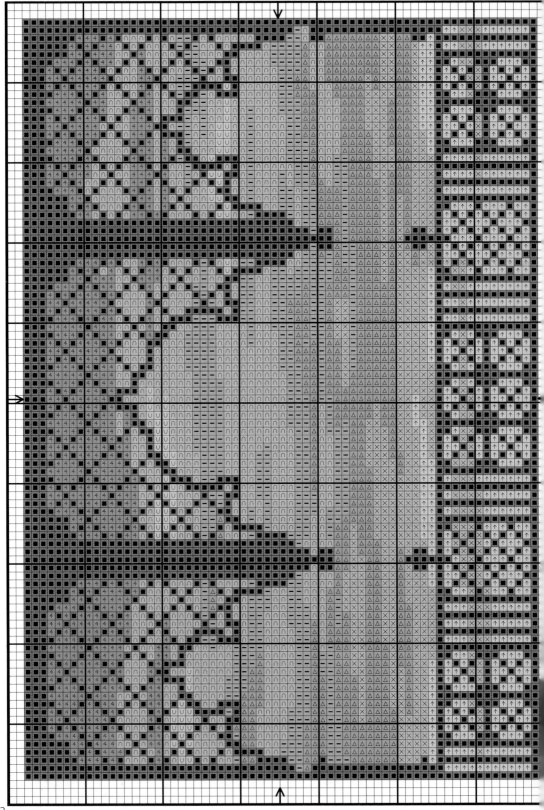

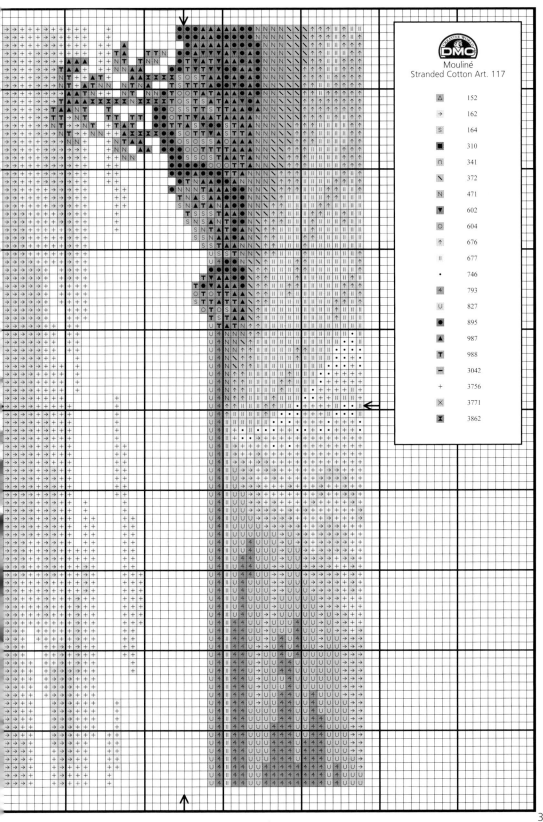

DMC CREATIVE WORLD
Mouliné
Stranded Cotton Art. 117

Symbol	Color
△	152
→	162
S	164
▣	310
n	341
＼	372
N	471
▼	602
O	604
↑	676
‖	677
•	746
4	793
U	827
●	895
▲	987
T	988
−	3042
+	3756
×	3771
⊠	3862

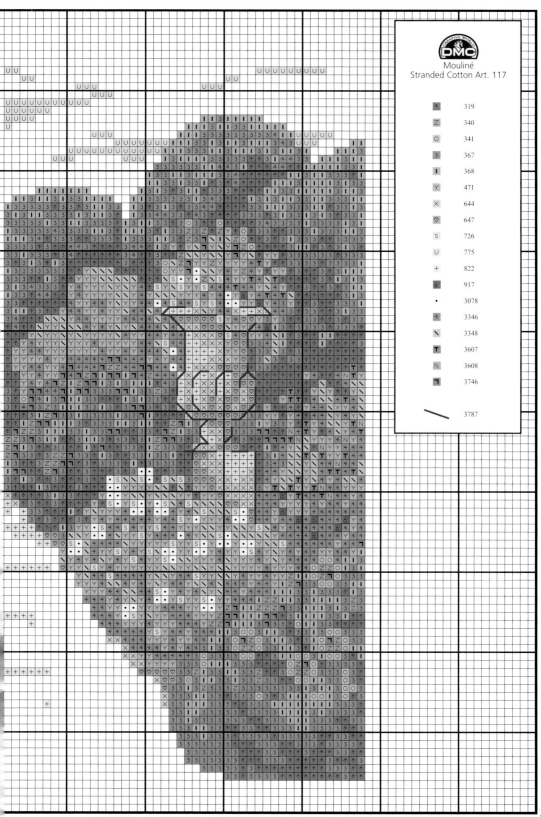

↑	319
Z	340
O	341
3	367
I	368
Y	471
X	644
♡	647
S	726
U	775
+	822
⊗	917
•	3078
4	3346
╲	3348
T	3607
N	3608
⌐	3746
╱	3787

Mouliné
Stranded Cotton Art. 117

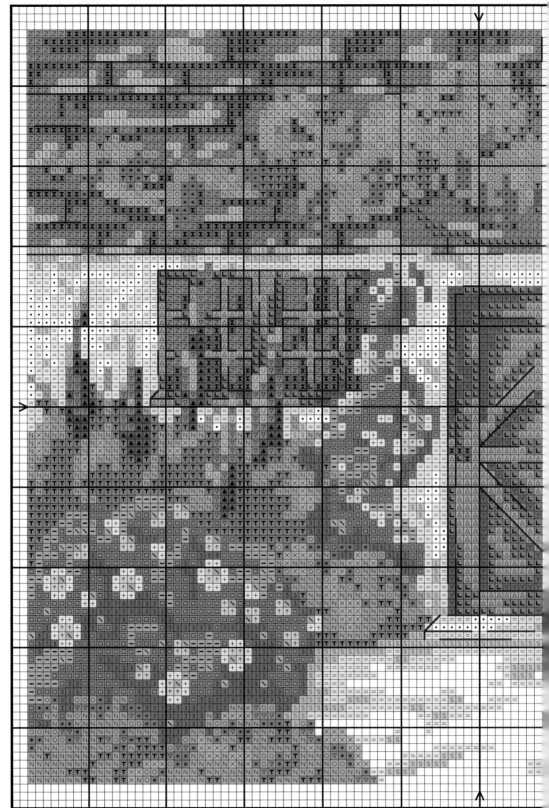

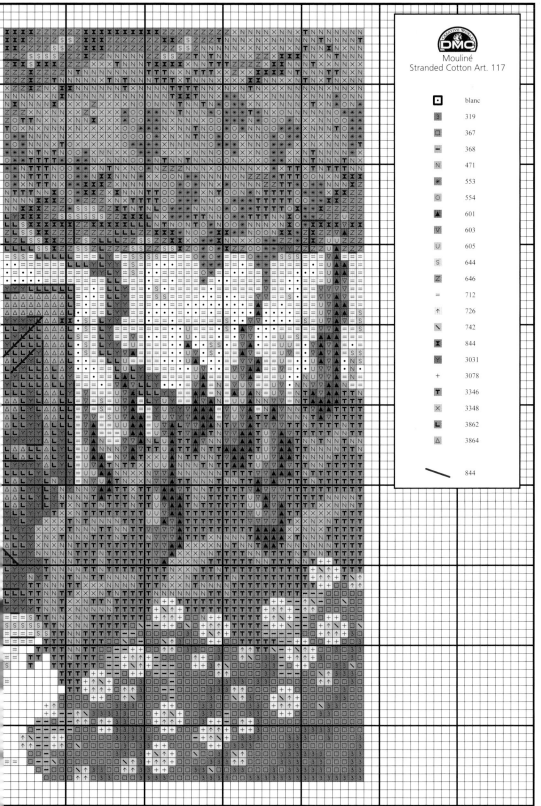

Mouliné
Stranded Cotton Art. 117

▣	blanc
3	319
▢	367
—	368
N	471
✳	553
O	554
▲	601
▽	603
U	605
S	644
Z	646
=	712
↑	726
◣	742
✗	844
✕	3031
+	3078
T	3346
✕	3348
L	3862
△	3864
╱	844

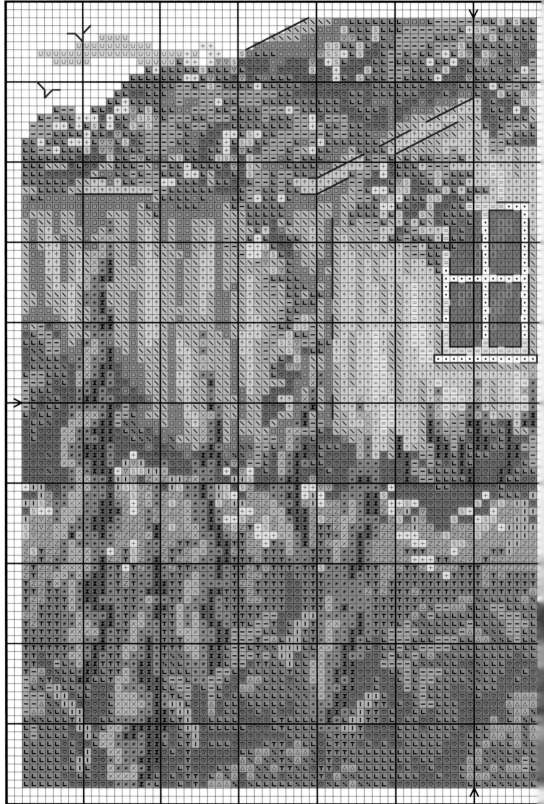

·	blanc
%	208
△	210
♡	319
L	367
−	368
Z	471
X	601
*	603
×	605
8	645
=	712
S	726
↑	739
▽	742
U	775
\	842
Y	844
+	3078
T	3346
I	3348
□	3863
/	844

Mouliné
Stranded Cotton Art. 117

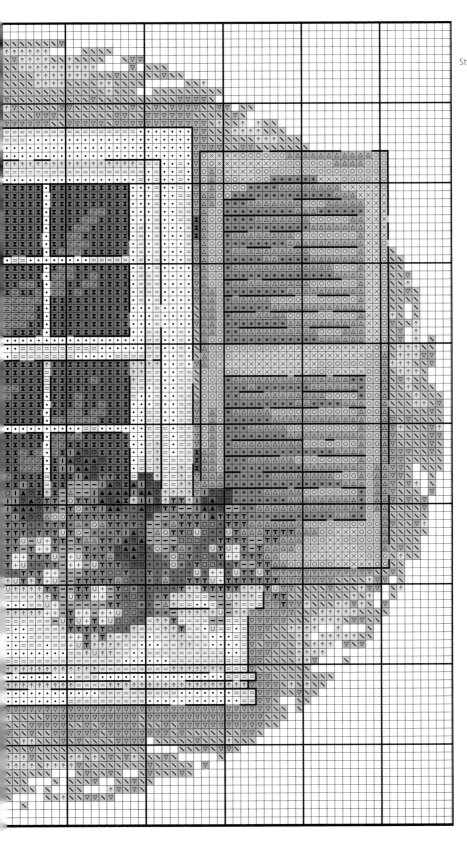

Mouliné
Stranded Cotton Art. 117

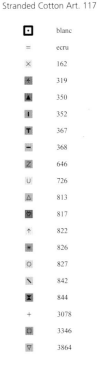

▣	blanc
=	ecru
✕	162
⊞	319
▲	350
Ⅰ	352
T	367
━	368
Z	646
U	726
△	813
▨	817
↑	822
✱	826
O	827
＼	842
✖	844
+	3078
▢	3346
▽	3864
╱	844

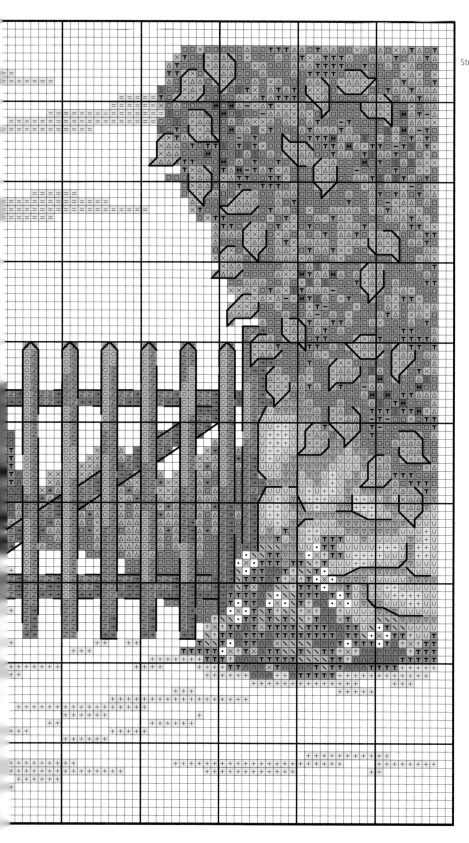

Mouliné
Stranded Cotton Art. 117

▣	blanc
✴	208
I	209
↑	211
∩	319
▨	350
–	352
T	367
╲	368
→	433
Z	435
○	437
△	471
▽	642
U	644
=	775
⋈	817
+	822
▤	3031
▢	3346
✕	3348

╲ 3031

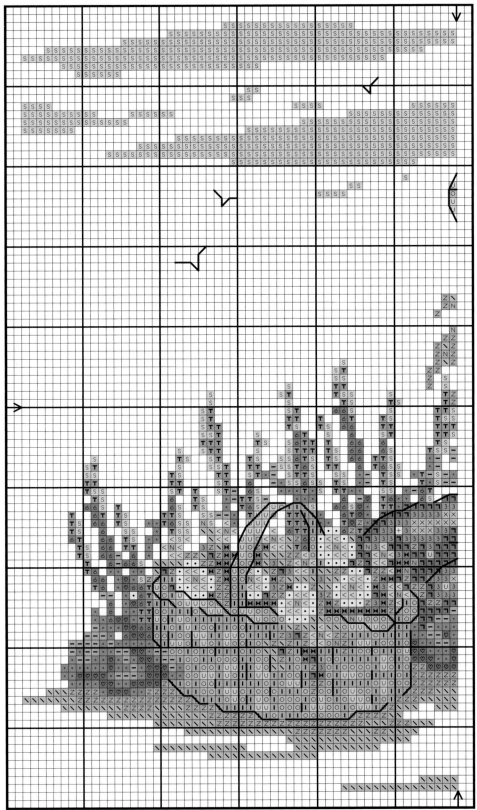

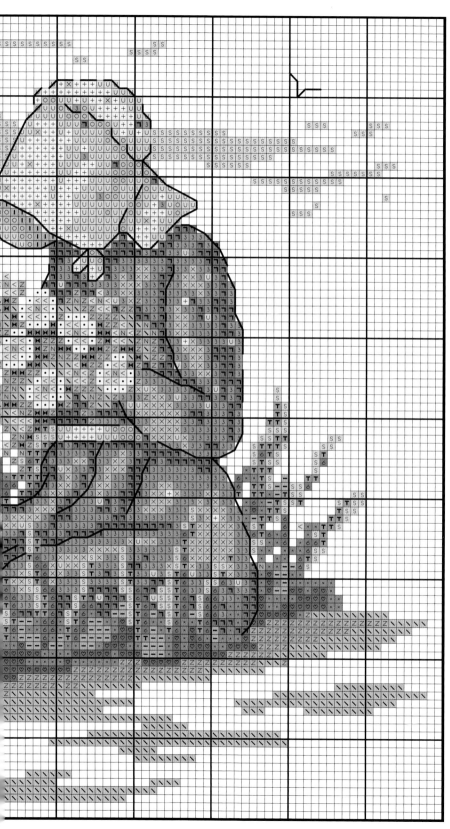

Mouliné
Stranded Cotton Art. 117

♡	319
T	340
✕	367
−	368
I	422
Z	471
+	712
<	726
N	742
O	3046
U	3047
•	3078
⋈	3346
⟍	3348
⅂	3687
3	3688
✕	3689
6	3746
S	3747
╱	3031

		DMC CREATIVE WORLD
		Mouliné Stranded Cotton Art. 117
U	162	
⋈	319	
⌐	367	
N	368	
I	471	
Z	642	
S	644	
⊗	777	
△	813	
•	819	
+	822	
3	826	
↑	963	
4	3031	
I	3046	
I	3047	
◇	3346	
×	3348	
T	3731	
N	3831	
−	3833	
◎	3862	
╱	3031	

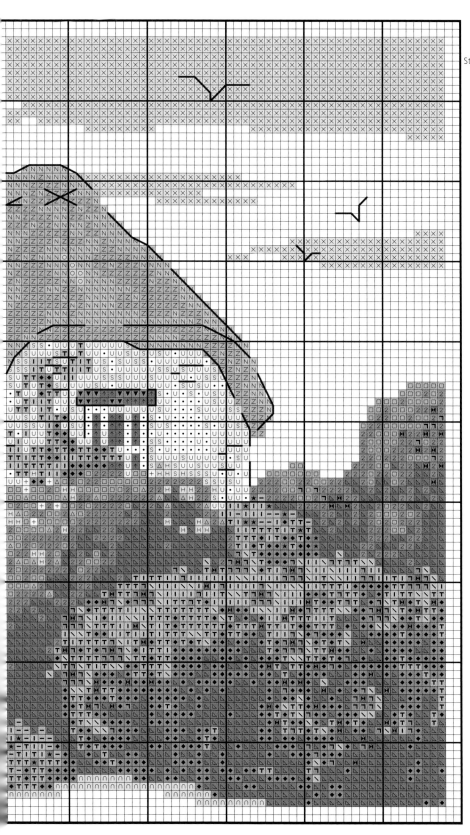

Mouliné
Stranded Cotton Art. 117

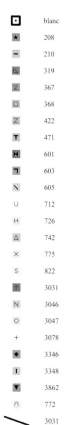

Symbol	Color
▣	blanc
★	208
─	210
◨	319
⊠	367
□	368
Z	422
T	471
◪	601
⅂	603
◥	605
U	712
H	726
△	742
×	775
S	822
⍓	3031
N	3046
O	3047
+	3078
◆	3346
I	3348
▼	3862
∩	772
╱	3031

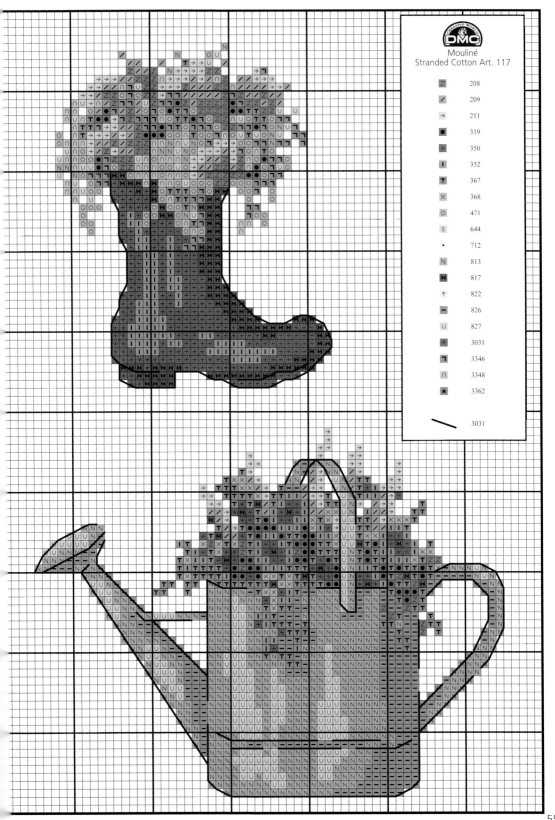

DMC
Mouliné
Stranded Cotton Art. 117

Symbol	Colour
Z	208
/	209
→	211
●	319
⊞	350
I	352
T	367
X	368
O	471
S	644
·	712
N	813
⋈	817
↑	822
—	826
U	827
4	3031
⌐	3346
∩	3348
★	3362
╱	3031

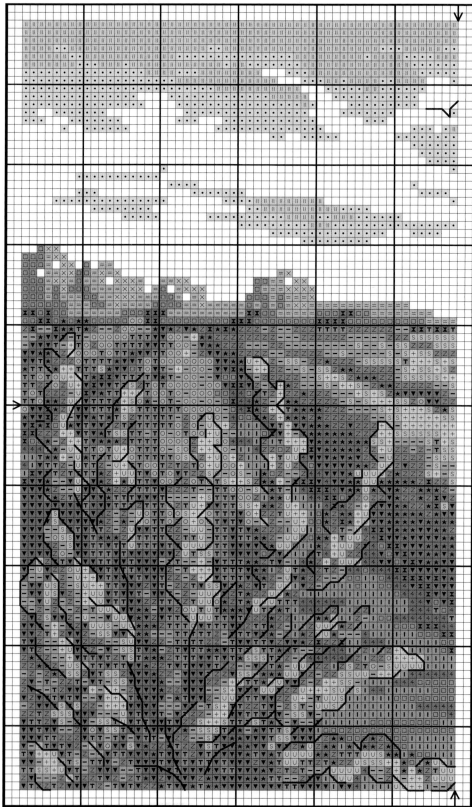

Mouliné
Stranded Cotton Art. 117

★	158
+	211
▼	319
−	340
S	341
T	367
O	368
=	471
•	775
✖	934
4	3031
II	3325
▢	3346
✕	3348
Z	3746
U	3840
I	3863

| / | 3031 |

DMC
Mouliné
Stranded Cotton Art. 117

Symbol	Number
⋈	319
⌐	367
N	368
T	435
−	471
U	726
○	742
+	775
I	926
⟍	927
→	928
✦	934
•	3078
=	3346
✕	3348
▲	3862
╱	3031

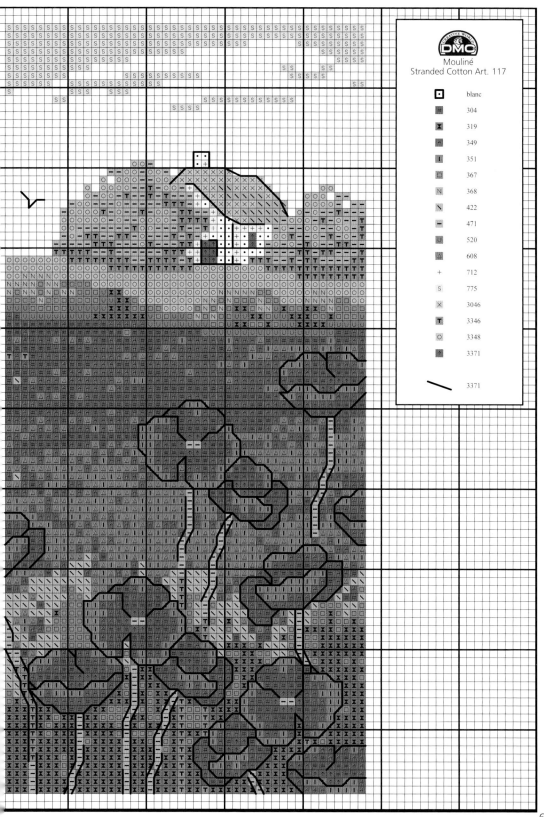

DMC
Mouliné
Stranded Cotton Art. 117

⊡	blanc
⊞	304
✕	319
⊞	349
I	351
⊡	367
N	368
\	422
⊟	471
U	520
◪	608
+	712
S	775
✕	3046
T	3346
O	3348
◪	3371
╱	3371

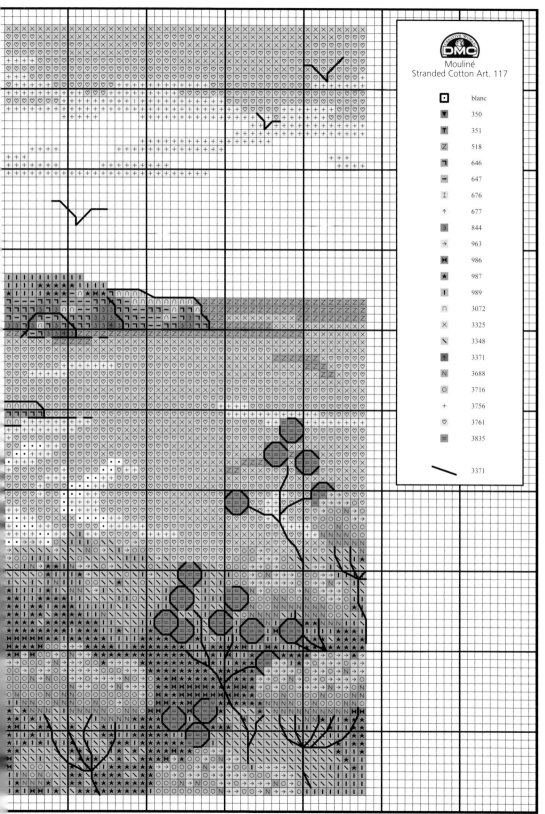

DMC
Mouliné
Stranded Cotton Art. 117

▣	blanc
▼	350
▼	351
Z	518
⌐	646
▬	647
I	676
↑	677
3	844
→	963
⋈	986
★	987
I	989
∩	3072
✕	3325
◥	3348
⊹	3371
N	3688
O	3716
+	3756
♡	3761
▬	3835
╱	3371

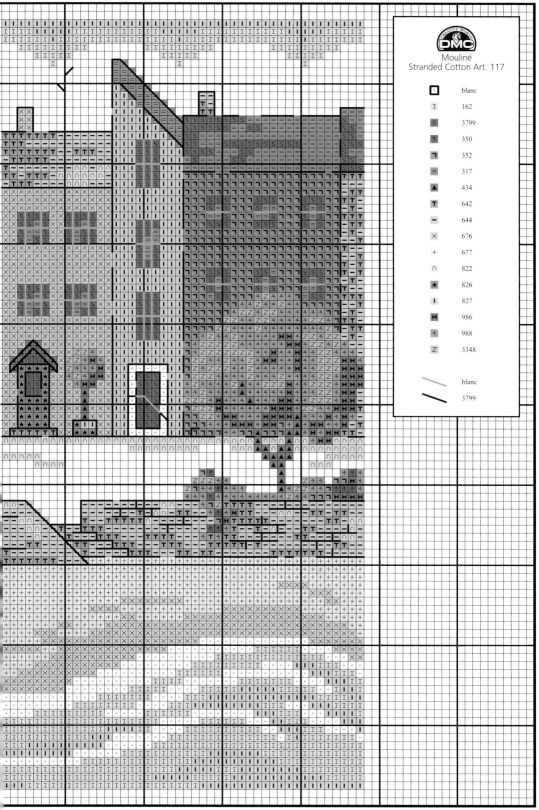

	blanc
I	162
S	3799
⋈	350
⌐	352
≡	317
▲	434
T	642
–	644
✕	676
+	677
∩	822
★	826
I	827
⋈	986
4	988
Z	3348

	blanc
	3799

Mouliné
Stranded Cotton Art. 117

DMC

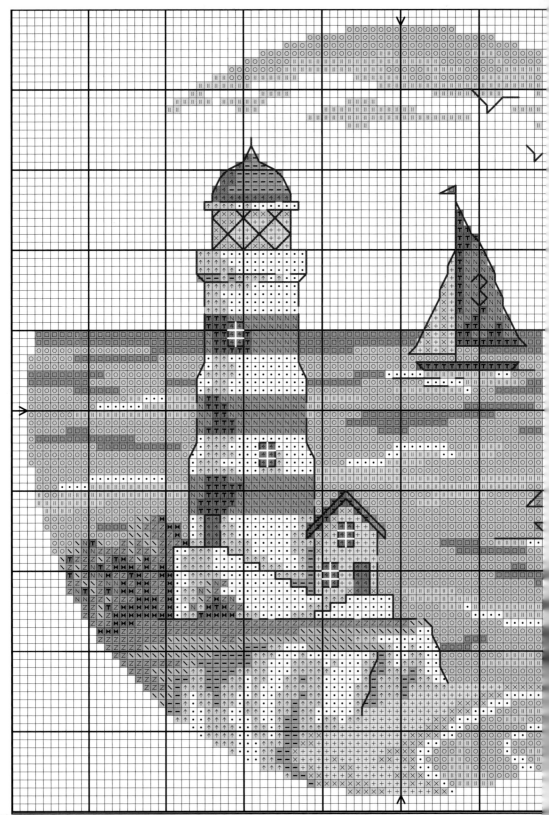

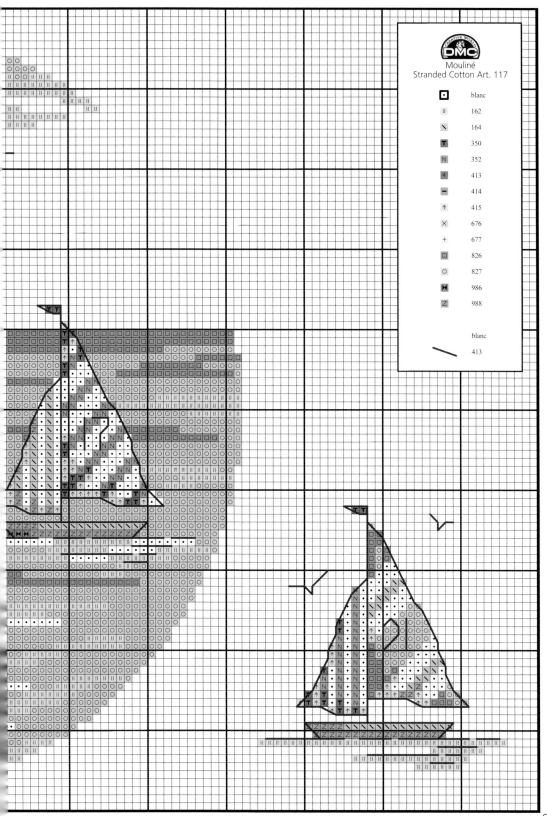

DMC
Mouliné
Stranded Cotton Art. 117

■	blanc	
II	162	
\	164	
T	350	
N	352	
4	413	
−	414	
↑	415	
X	676	
+	677	
▢	826	
O	827	
⋈	986	
Z	988	

blanc

413

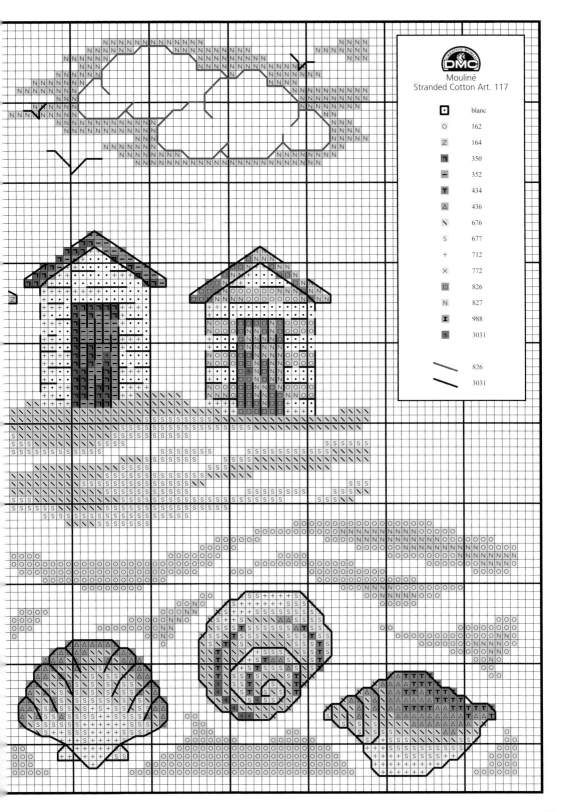

DMC
Mouliné
Stranded Cotton Art. 117

	blanc
O	162
Z	164
	350
–	352
T	434
△	436
\	676
S	677
+	712
×	772
⊡	826
N	827
X	988
4	3031
	826
	3031

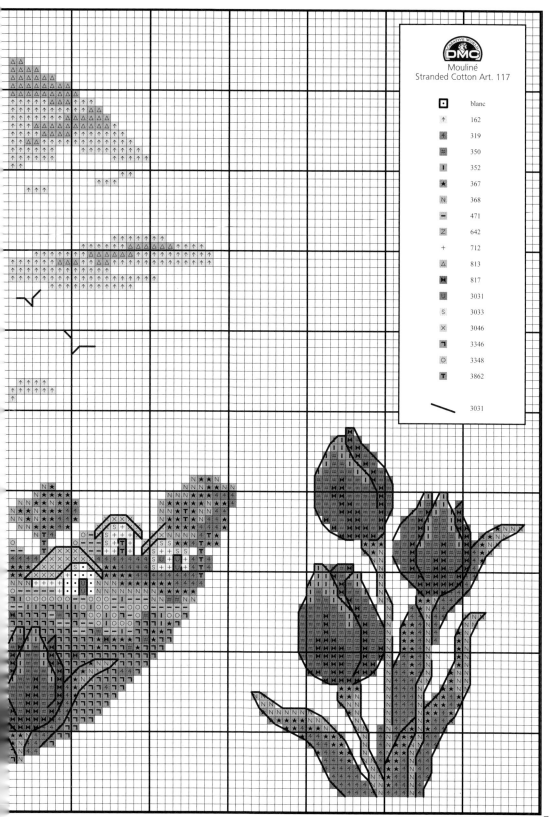

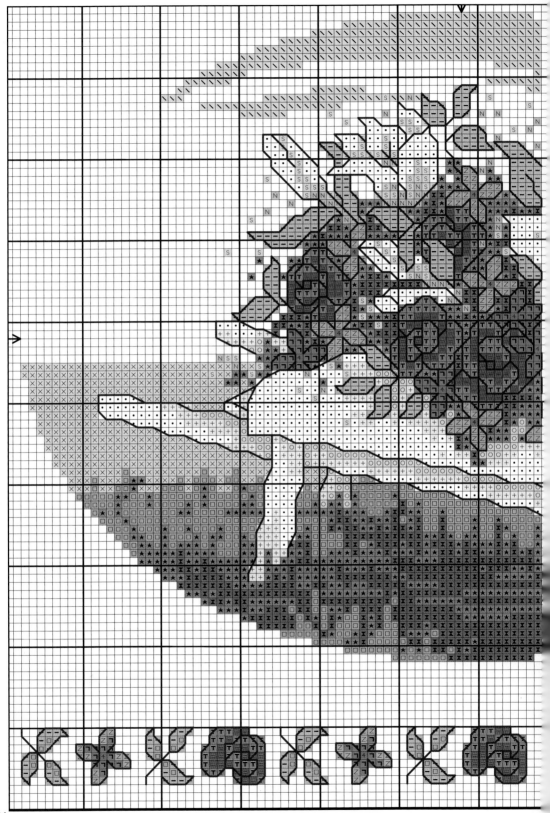

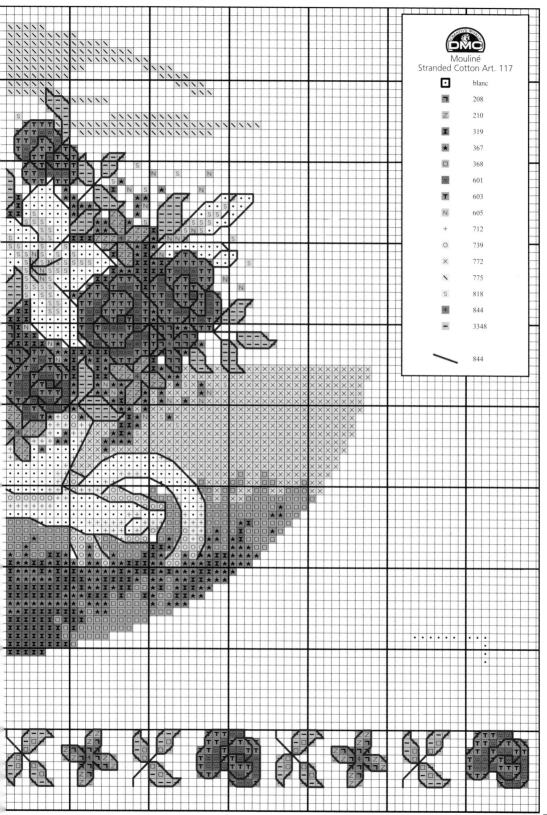

DMC
Mouliné
Stranded Cotton Art. 117

Symbol	Color
▣	blanc
㇉	208
Z	210
✕	319
★	367
▢	368
▦	601
T	603
N	605
+	712
O	739
×	772
＼	775
S	818
+	844
−	3348
╱	844

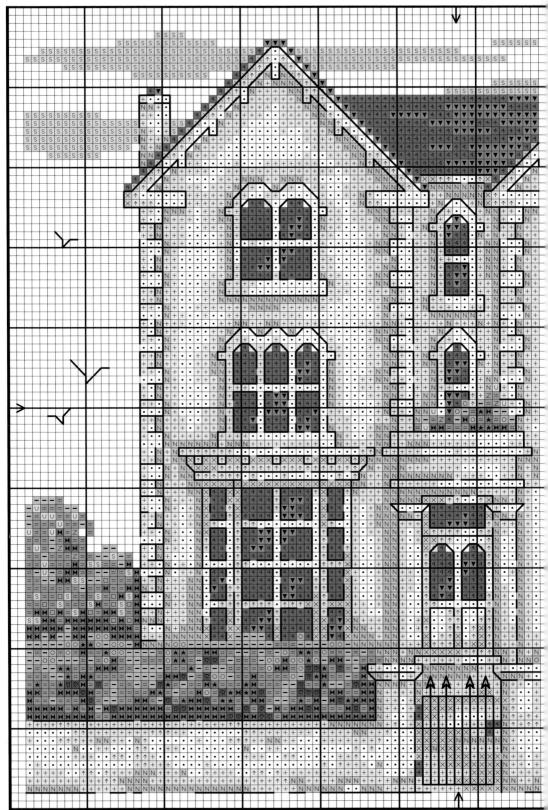

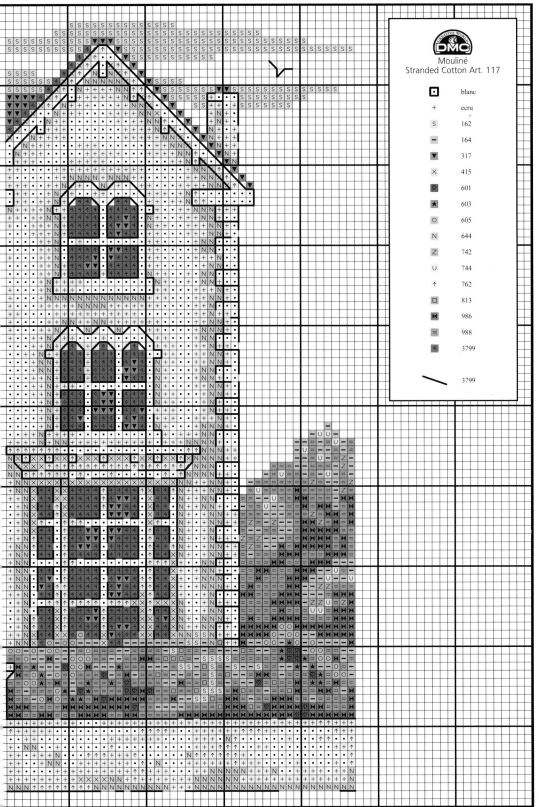

DMC
Mouliné
Stranded Cotton Art. 117

⊡	blanc
+	ecru
S	162
▬	164
▼	317
✕	415
▨	601
★	603
○	605
N	644
Z	742
U	744
↑	762
▢	813
▨	986
▤	988
◢	3799
╱	3799

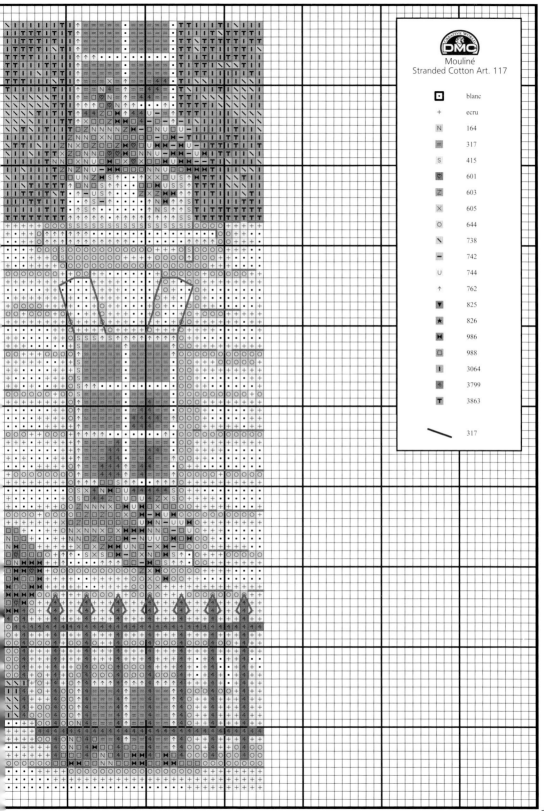

DMC
Mouliné
Stranded Cotton Art. 117

⊡	blanc
+	ecru
N	164
⚌	317
S	415
♥	601
Z	603
X	605
O	644
\	738
–	742
U	744
↑	762
▼	825
★	826
⋈	986
□	988
I	3064
4	3799
T	3863

⟋ 317

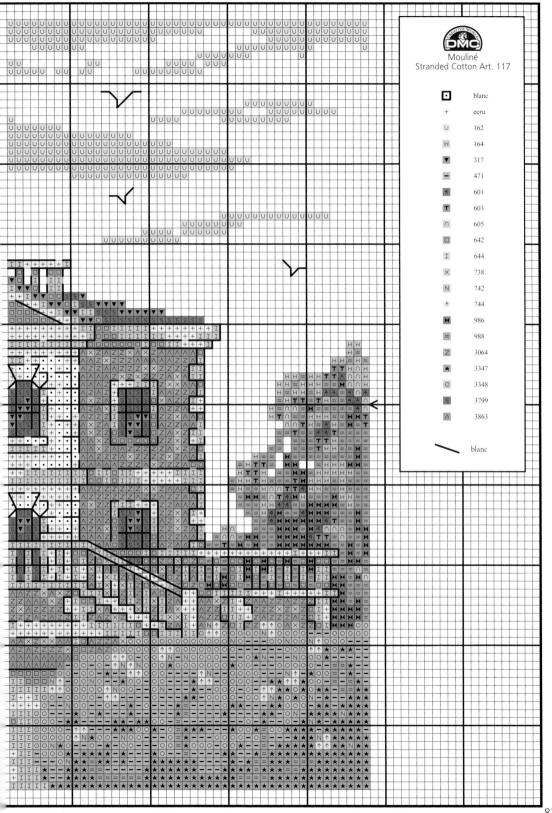

Mouliné
Stranded Cotton Art. 117

▣	blanc
+	ecru
U	162
H	164
▼	317
⊟	471
⋈	601
T	603
∩	605
▢	642
I	644
✕	738
N	742
↑	744
⋈	986
⊞	988
Z	3064
★	3347
O	3348
S	3799
∧	3863
╲	blanc

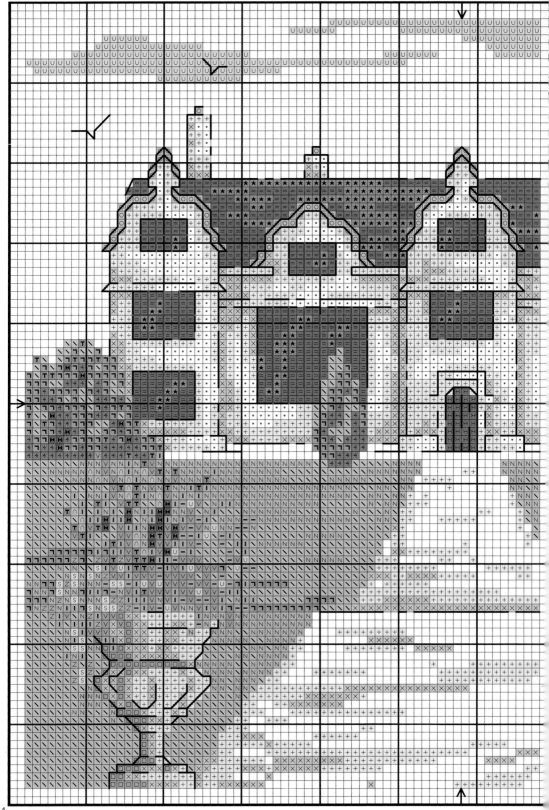

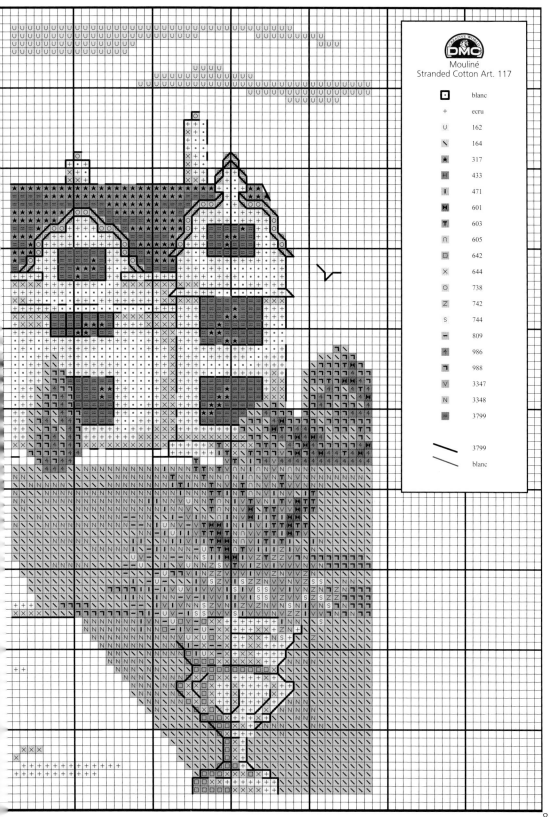

DMC
Mouliné
Stranded Cotton Art. 117

▣	blanc
+	ecru
U	162
╲	164
★	317
H	433
I	471
ꓱ	601
T	603
⋒	605
▢	642
×	644
O	738
Z	742
S	744
━	809
⨮	986
⅂	988
V	3347
N	3348
═	3799
╱	3799
╱	blanc

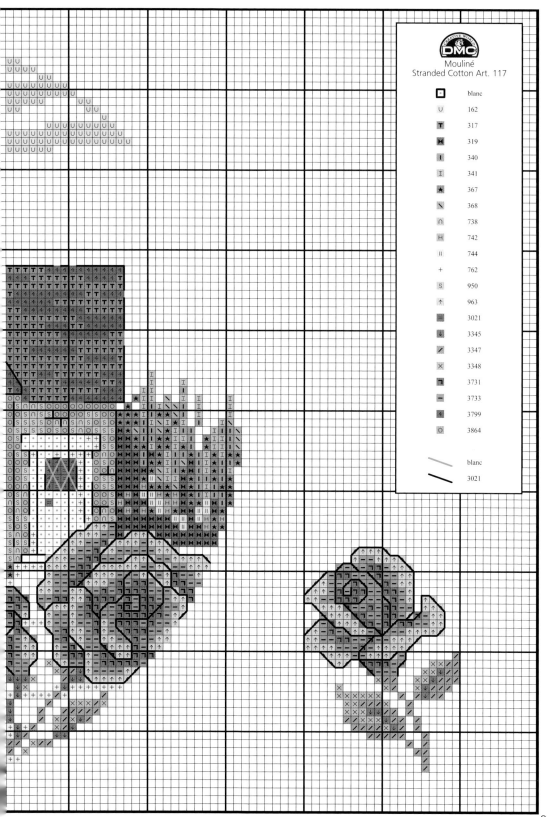

DMC
Mouliné
Stranded Cotton Art. 117

▢	blanc
U	162
Ŧ	317
Ħ	319
▮	340
I	341
★	367
＼	368
∩	738
H	742
‖	744
+	762
S	950
↑	963
⊟	3021
↓	3345
╱	3347
✕	3348
◪	3731
—	3733
✦	3799
○	3864
╱	blanc
╱	3021

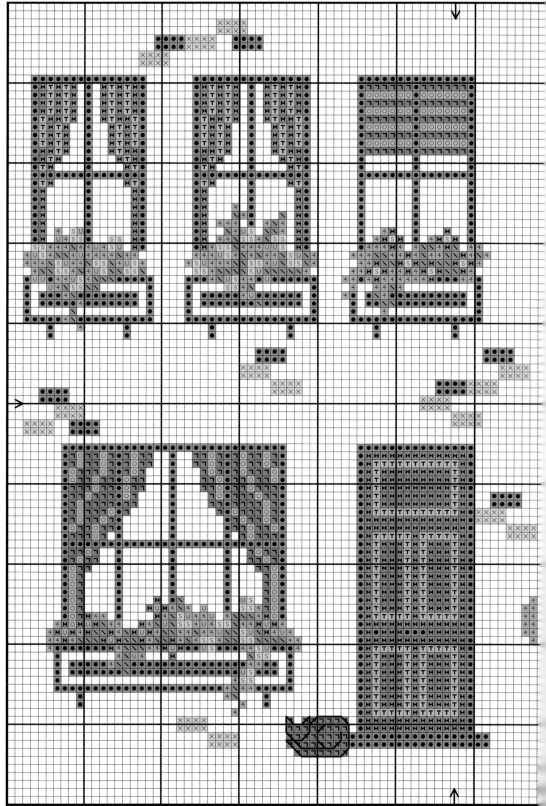

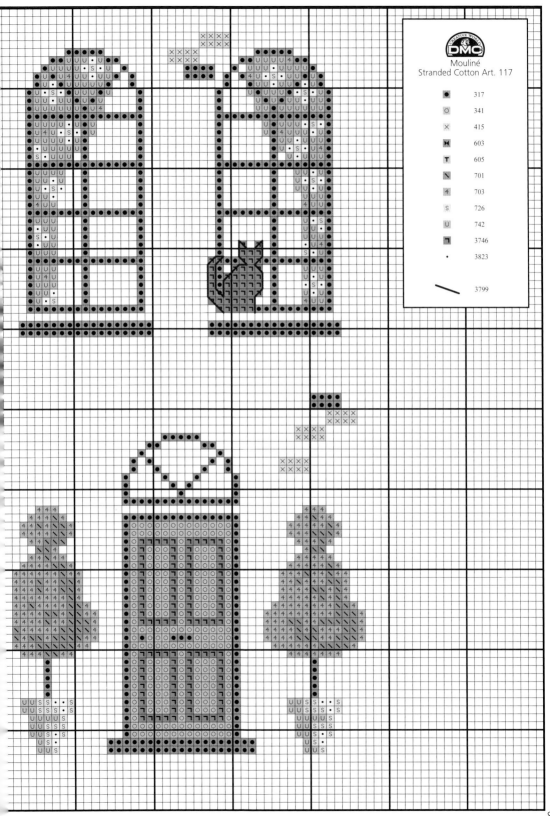

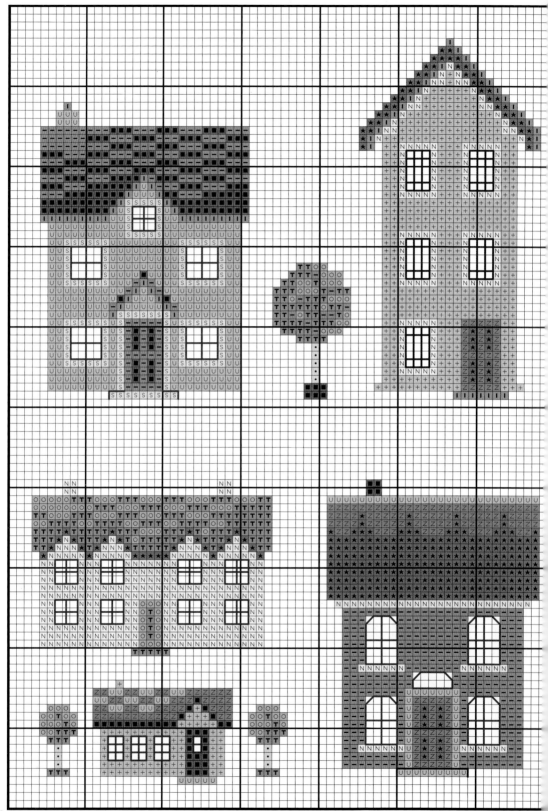

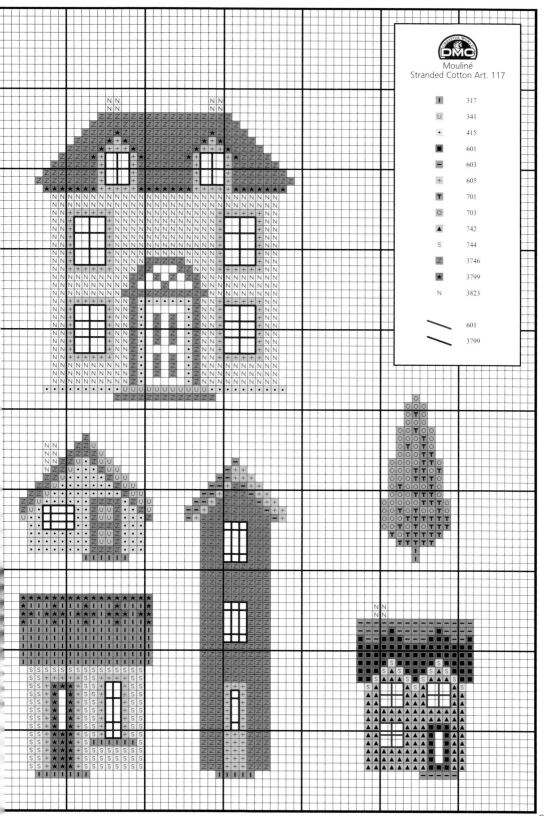

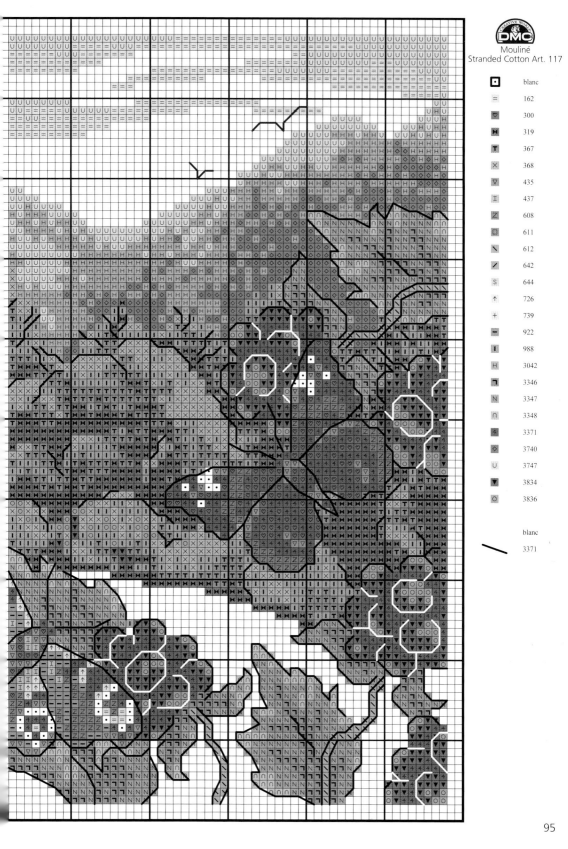

⊡	blanc
▼	300
∩	316
I	334
↑	341
<	437
▮	606
N	608
‖	726
+	745
3	803
★	817
T	919
✕	922
▢	935
▬	987
○	989
S	3340
4	3371
Z	3721
●	3857
△	3862

Mouliné
Stranded Cotton Art. 117

╱ 3371

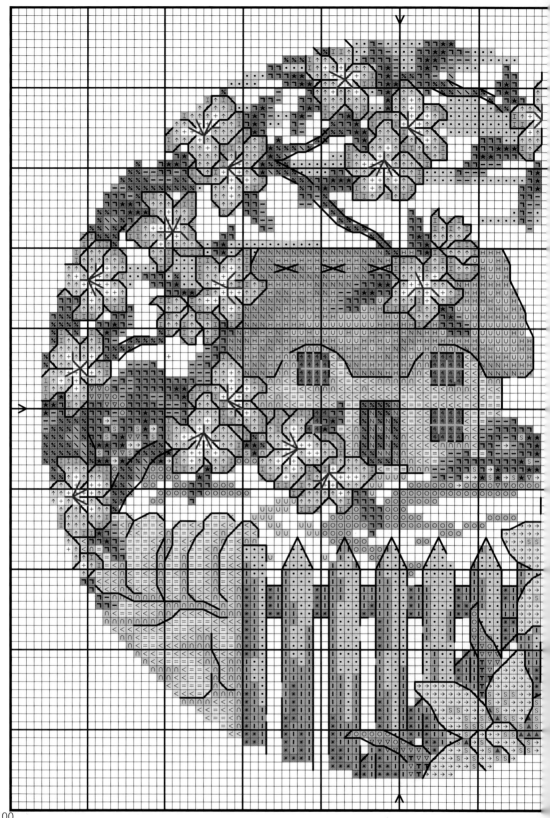

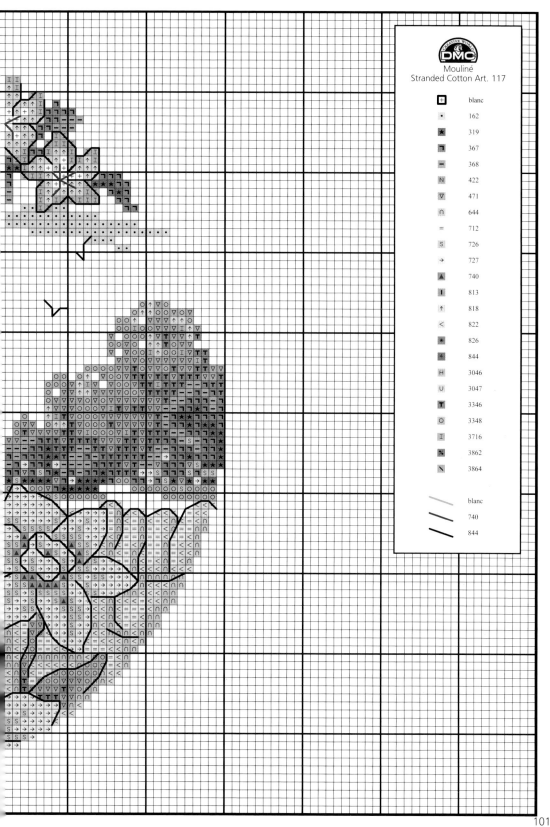

	Mouliné
	Stranded Cotton Art. 117
⊞	blanc
•	162
★	319
⌐	367
−	368
N	422
▽	471
∩	644
=	712
S	726
→	727
▲	740
I	813
↑	818
<	822
✳	826
✦	844
H	3046
U	3047
T	3346
O	3348
I	3716
✕	3862
◣	3864
╱	blanc
╱	740
╱	844

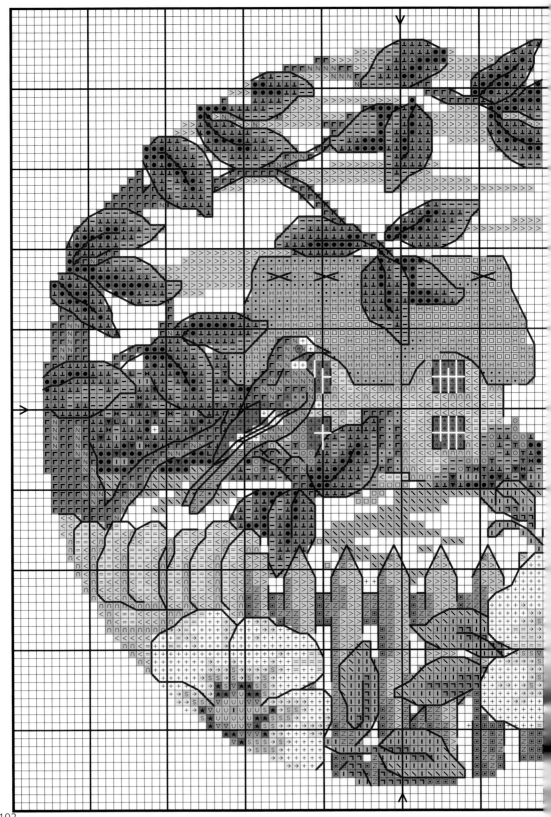

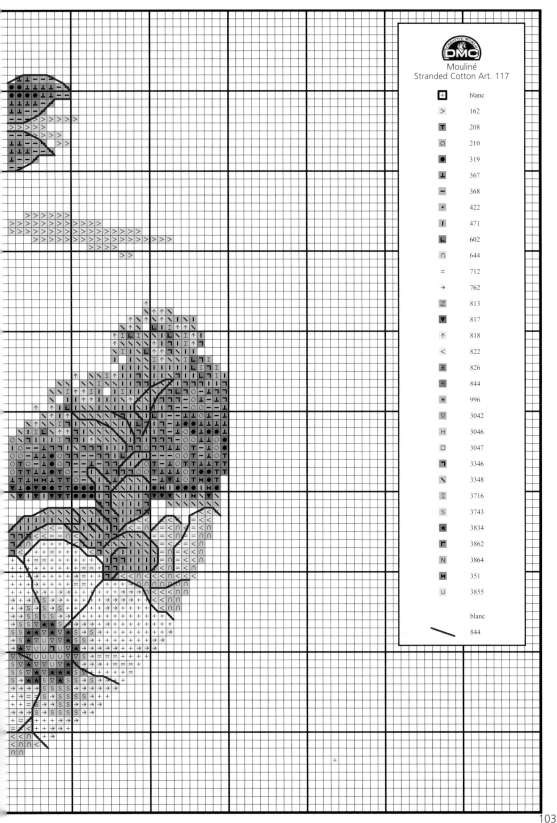

DMC
Mouliné
Stranded Cotton Art. 117

⊞	blanc
>	162
⊤	208
○	210
●	319
⊥	367
⊢	368
•	422
ꛁ	471
⫿	602
∩	644
=	712
→	762
Z	813
▼	817
↑	818
<	822
▣	826
◿	844
✳	996
▽	3042
H	3046
□	3047
◲	3346
＼	3348
꛱	3716
S	3743
★	3834
⌐	3862
N	3864
⋈	351
U	3855
	blanc
╱	844

103

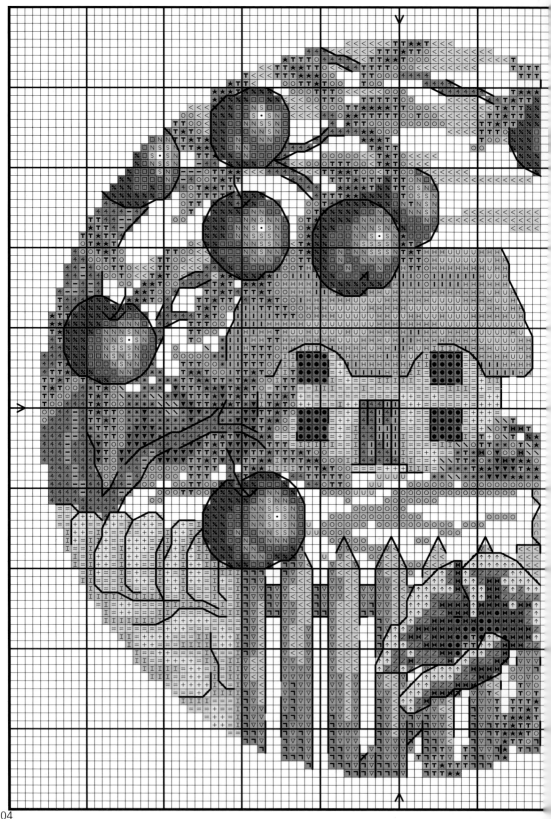

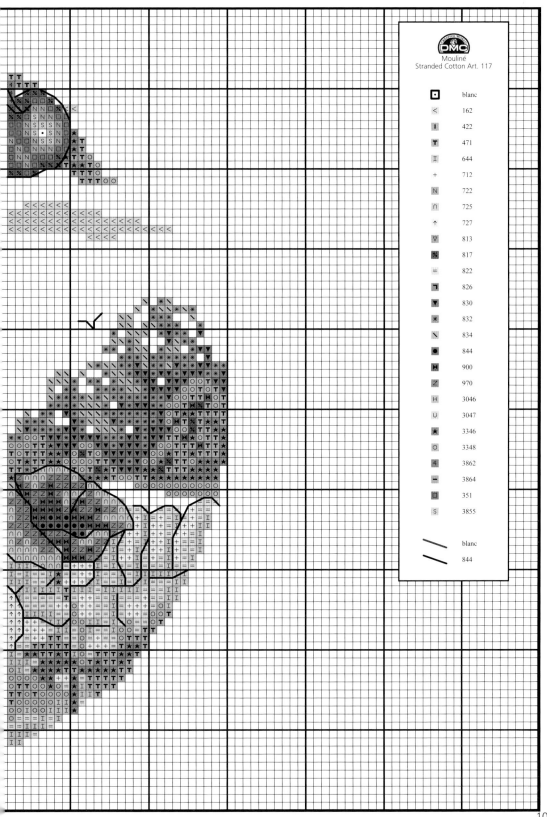

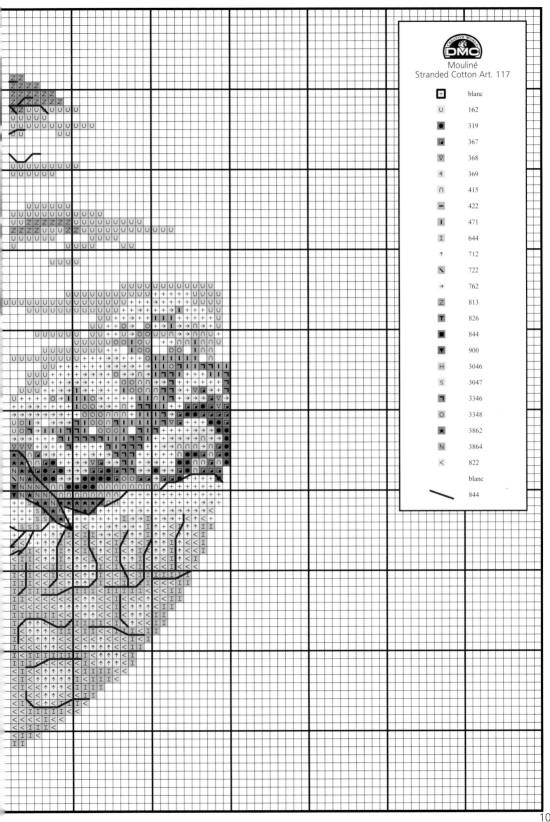

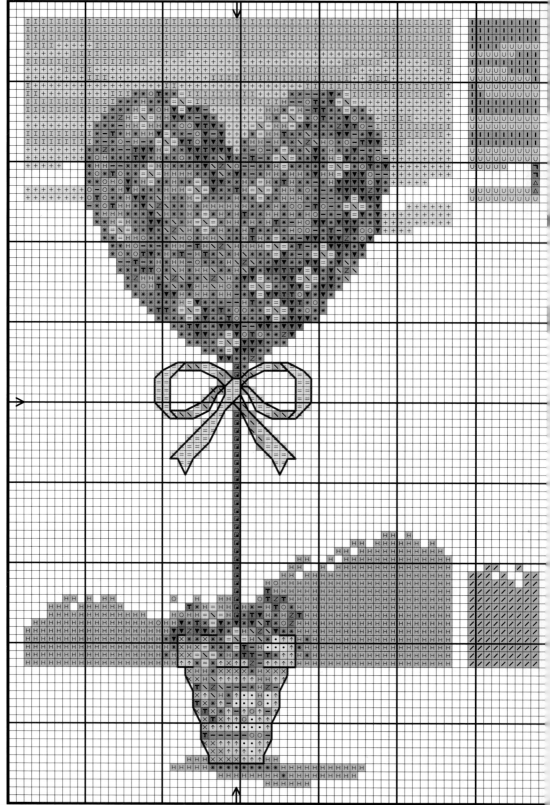

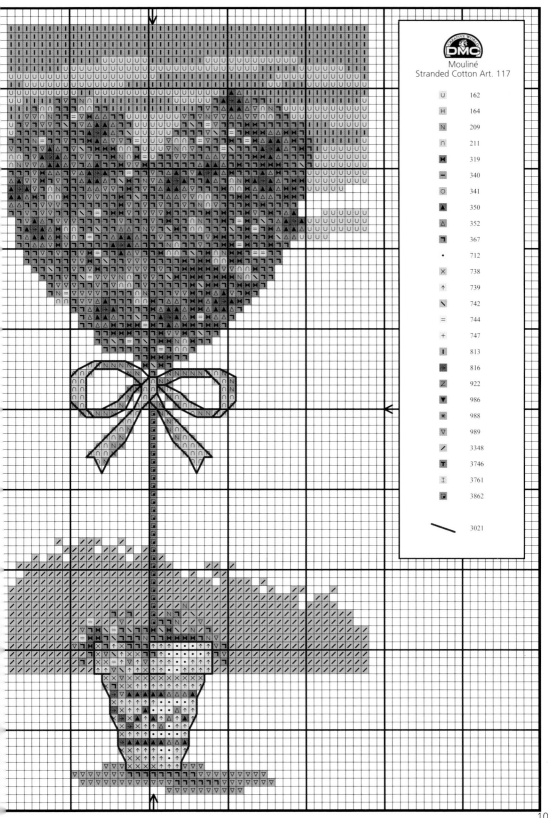

DMC
Mouliné
Stranded Cotton Art. 117

Symbol	Number
U	162
H	164
N	209
∩	211
⋈	319
−	340
○	341
▲	350
△	352
⅂	367
•	712
×	738
↑	739
\	742
=	744
+	747
I	813
✳	816
Z	922
▼	986
✳	988
▽	989
╱	3348
T	3746
I	3761
▣	3862
╱	3021

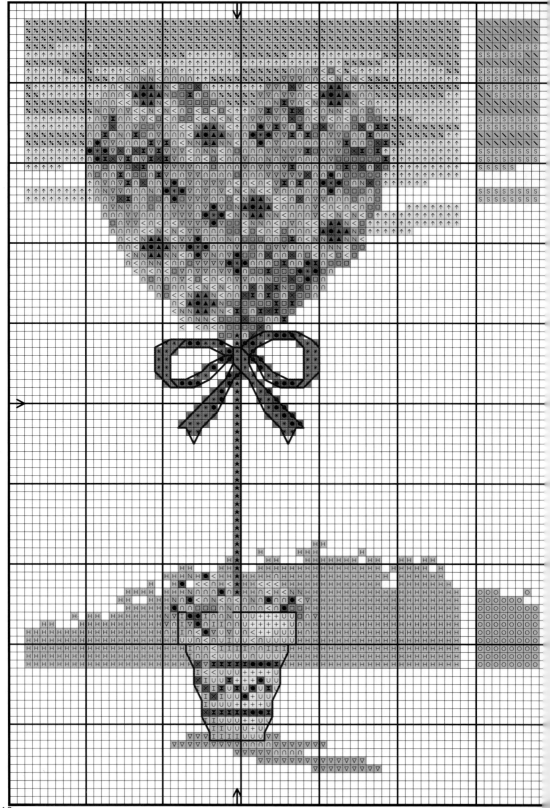

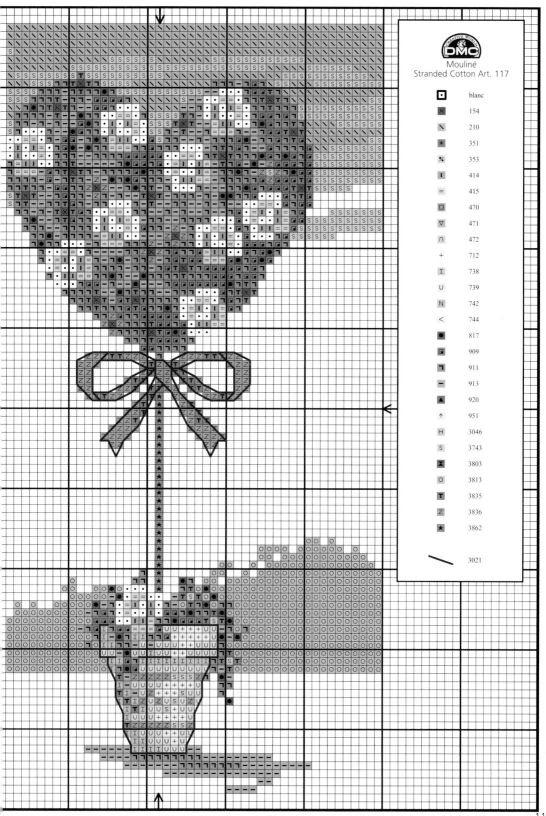

DMC
CREATIVE WORLD
Mouliné
Stranded Cotton Art. 117

⊡	blanc
☒	154
＼	210
＊	351
％	353
Ｉ	414
＝	415
▣	470
▽	471
∩	472
＋	712
Ｉ	738
Ｕ	739
Ｎ	742
＜	744
●	817
▣	909
ㄱ	911
－	913
▲	920
↑	951
Ｈ	3046
Ｓ	3743
☒	3803
○	3813
Ｔ	3835
Ｚ	3836
★	3862
╲	3021